89 Organic Lung Cancer Salad and Meal Recipes:

These Salads and Meals Will Strengthen Your Immune System through Powerful Superfood Sources

By

Joe Correa CSN

COPYRIGHT

© 2019 Live Stronger Faster Inc.

All rights reserved

Reproduction or translation of any part of this work beyond that permitted by section 107 or 108 of the 1976 United States Copyright Act without the permission of the copyright owner is unlawful.

This publication is designed to provide accurate and authoritative information in regard to the subject matter covered. It is sold with the understanding that neither the author nor the publisher is engaged in rendering medical advice. If medical advice or assistance is needed, consult with a doctor. This book is considered a guide and should not be used in any way detrimental to your health. Consult with a physician before starting this nutritional plan to make sure it's right for you.

ACKNOWLEDGEMENTS

This book is dedicated to my friends and family that have had mild or serious illnesses so that you may find a solution and make the necessary changes in your life.

89 Organic Lung Cancer Salad and Meal Recipes:

These Salads and Meals Will Strengthen Your Immune System through Powerful Superfood Sources

By

Joe Correa CSN

CONTENTS

Copyright

Acknowledgements

About The Author

Introduction

Commitment

89 Organic Lung Cancer Salad and Meal Recipes: These Salads and Meals Will Strengthen Your Immune System through Powerful Superfood Sources

Additional Titles from This Author

ABOUT THE AUTHOR

After years of Research, I honestly believe in the positive effects that proper nutrition can have over the body and mind. My knowledge and experience has helped me live healthier throughout the years and which I have shared with family and friends. The more you know about eating and drinking healthier, the sooner you will want to change your life and eating habits.

Nutrition is a key part in the process of being healthy and living longer so get started today. The first step is the most important and the most significant.

INTRODUCTION

89 Organic Lung Cancer Salad and Meal Recipes: These Salads and Meals Will Strengthen Your Immune System through Powerful Superfood Sources

By Joe Correa CSN

Lung cancer is the leading cause of "cancer deaths" in the world. In order to realize the true seriousness of lung cancer, you have to understand that it takes more lives than colon, prostate, ovarian, and breast cancer combined.

The highest known risk factor of lung cancer is definitely smoking. Other factors include secondhand smoke, exposure to radon gas, and exposure to asbestos or other similar carcinogens.

Naturally, the best way to reduce the risk of lung cancer is to stop smoking and avoid secondhand smoke. Even if you have been smoking for years, this will significantly reduce the risk of lung cancer. Talk to your doctor about different strategies to help you quit.

Eating plenty of fruit and vegetables will provide your body with a good amount of vitamins and nutrients which will then help your body improve its own defense mechanisms. Some research suggests that beta carotene, among other nutrients, can help reduce the risk of lung cancer, especially in smokers.

This book is a great collection of healthy and delicious recipes that are based on what your body needs the most, nutritionally loaded raw ingredients that will improve your health and keep you full for hours.

COMMITMENT

In order to improve my condition, I *(your name)*, commit to eating more of these foods on a daily basis and to exercise at least 30 minutes daily:

- Berries (especially blueberries), peaches, cherries, apples, apricots, oranges, lemon juice, grapefruit, tangerines, mandarins, pears, etc.
- Broccoli, spinach, collard greens, sweet potatoes, avocado, artichoke, baby corn, carrots, celery, cauliflower, onions, etc.
- Whole grains, steel-cut oats, oatmeal, quinoa, barley, etc.
- Black beans, red bean beans, garbanzo beans, lentils, etc.
- Nuts and seeds including: walnuts, cashews, flaxseeds, sesame seeds, etc.
- Fish
- 8 – 10 glasses of water

Sign here

X_____

89 ORGANIC LUNG CANCER SALAD AND MEAL RECIPES: THESE SALADS AND MEALS WILL STRENGTHEN YOUR IMMUNE SYSTEM THROUGH POWERFUL SUPERFOOD SOURCES

SALAD RECIPES

1. **Sweet Potato and Walnut Salad**

Ingredients:

1 medium sweet potato, cut into chunks

2 eggs, hard-boiled

7oz chicken breast, boneless and skinless

1 medium onion, diced

3 garlic cloves, crushed

1oz walnuts, finely chopped

2 tbsp olive oil

1 tbsp parsley, finely chopped

Salt and freshly ground black pepper to taste

Preparation:

Rinse potatoes thoroughly under cold running water. Pat dry and place on a clean work surface. Using a sharp knife, cut into bite-sized pieces and add to a deep, heavy-bottomed pan. Pour in enough water to cover and sprinkle with some salt.

Bring potatoes to a boil and cook until fork tender. When done, remove from the heat and drain. Set aside to cool.

Meanwhile, add eggs to a pot of boiling water and cook for 12 minutes. Remove from the heat and drain. Cool to a room temperature and then peel. Slice eggs and transfer to a serving bowl along with potatoes. Set aside.

Now, peel and chop onions. Add to a bowl along with crushed garlic. Sprinkle with one tablespoon of olive oil, parsley, salt, pepper, and walnuts. Mix all well and set aside.

Rinse the meat under cold running water and pat dry with a kitchen towel. Place ona a cutting board and chop into bite-sized pieces.

Grease a medium pan with the remaining oil and preheat over medium-high heat. Add the meat and sprinkle with some salt. Pour in about ¼ cup of water and cover with the lid. Cook, covered, for 15 minutes.

Remove the lid and continue to cook until all the liquid has evaporated. Cool for a while and serve over the prepared salad.

Nutritional information per serving: Kcal: 464, Protein: 32.1g, Carbs: 20.3g, Fats: 29.4g

2. Black Bean and Buckwheat Salad

Ingredients:

1 cup buckwheat groats

1 ripe avocado, sliced

1 small purple onion, diced

2 cups spinach, chopped

1 cup black beans, drained

1 cucumber

2 tbsp lime juice

2 tbsp olive oil

2 tbsp sesame seeds

1 tbsp honey

½ tsp cumin powder

1 small chili, diced

Salt and pepper to taste

Preparation:

Add buckwheat to a small pan and pour in 2 cups of water. Bring to a boil and reduce the heat to medium. Gently simmer for 10-15 minutes or until buckwheat has absorbed all the liquid. Remove from the heat and set aside.

Meanwhile, prepare the vegetables. Rinse spinach under cold running water and drain in a large colander. Transfer to a bowl.

Peel and slice avocado, slice cucumber, and chop the onion. Transfer all to a serving bowl and add buckwheat and drained beans. Mix all well and set aside.

In a small bowl, whisk together lime juice, olive oil, sesame seeds, honey, cumin powder, diced chili, salt and pepper.

Pour the mixture over salad and stir well. Serve immediately.

Nutritional information per serving: Kcal: 410, Protein: 12.3g, Carbs: 50.2g, Fats: 20.9g

3. Tomato and Arugula Salad with Macadamia Nuts

Ingredients:

1 ripe tomato, cut into bite-sized pieces

2 small onions, diced

1 garlic clove, crushed

2 cups arugula, torn

2oz macadamia nuts, chopped

½ cup heavy cream

½ chicken stock cube

3 tbsp plain Greek yogurt

1 tsp lemon zest

Salt to taste

Preparation:

Wash tomato and slice into bite-sized pieces. Add to a bowl.

Peel and chop onions. Transfer to a medium sieve and generously sprinkle with salt. Let it sit for 10-12 minutes to remove the bitterness. Rinse thoroughly under cold running water and drain. Transfer to a bowl with tomato and add garlic and arugula. Set aside.

Add heavy cream to a small saucepan and gently heat up over medium heat. Add chicken stock cube, Greek yogurt, lemon zest, and some salt. Mix all well and cook for 2-3 minutes, stirring constantly.

Remove the mixture from the heat and cool to a room temperature.

Drizzle over salad and serve.

Nutritional information per serving: Kcal: 370, Protein: 7.6g, Carbs: 15.4g, Fats: 33.3g

4. Red Pepper Salad with Chicken and Pine Nuts

Ingredients:

7oz chicken breast, boneless and skinless

2 cups lettuce, chopped

1 red bell pepper, diced

½ cucumber, sliced

1oz pine nuts

3 tbsp plain Greek yogurt

2 tsp Worcestershire sauce

2 tbsp parsley, finely chopped

Salt

Preparation:

Preheat the oven to 400 degrees F. Line a small baking pan with some parchment paper and set aside.

Rinse the meat under cold running water and pat dry with a kitchen paper. Transfer to a cutting board and chop into bite-sized pieces. Set aside.

In a small bowl, mix together Greek yogurt, Worcestershire sauce, parsley, and salt. Sprinkle the meat with this mixture and bake for 15 minutes.

Remove the meat from the oven and cool to a room temperature.

Meanwhile, wash and prepare vegetables. Rinse lettuce under cold running water and add to serving bowl.

Wash the bell pepper and remove the stem. Slice in half, lenghtwise and remove the seeds. Rinse well again and slice into bite-sized pieces. Add to a bowl along with sliced cucumber and pine nuts.

Top with the meat and mix all well. Serve.

Nutritional information per serving: Kcal: 269, Protein: 25.7g, Carbs: 13.6g, Fats: 12.8g

5. Artichoke Salad Toast

Ingredients:

7oz artichoke spears, chopped into bite-sized pieces

2 garlic cloves, crushed

1 small onion, diced

½ avocado, sliced

1 tbsp olive oil

1oz raisins

Salt and pepper to taste

4 slices whole wheat toast bread

Preparation:

Grease a small skillet with olive oil and heat over medium heat. Add onions and garlic and saute until translucent, stirring constantly.

Now, add artichoke spears and cook for 5 minutes. Remove from the heat and cool for a while.

Meanwhile, peel and finely chop onions. Add to a bowl along with avocado, garlic, and raisins. Sprinkle with salt and pepper and add chilled artichoke spears. Set aside.

Lightly toast the bread and and serve with the prepared

artichoke mixture. Serve.

Nutritional information per serving: Kcal: 423, Protein: 13.4g, Carbs: 55.8g, Fats: 19.1g

6. Mexican Lentil Salad

Ingredients:

1 cup brown lentils, drained

¾ cup sweet corn, drained

½ cup black beans, drained

2 tbsp walnuts, finely chopped

1 celery stalk, sliced

1 medium onion, diced

1 cup cherry tomatoes, sliced

1 chili pepper, diced

2 tbsp parsley, finely chopped

1 tbsp olive oil

Salt

Preparation:

Rinse and drain lentils, corn, and black beans. Transfer to serving bowl and set aside.

Peel and finely chop onions. Add to a bowl.

Slice each cherry tomato in half, lenthgwise and add to a bowl along with the remaining ingredients. Mix all well and sprinkle with olive oil and salt.

Serve.

Nutritional information per serving: Kcal: 450, Protein: 21.8g, Carbs: 64.7g, Fats: 13.8g

7. Warm Kale Salad

Ingredients:

1 head kale, medium

1 pear, sliced

¼ cup dried cranberries

¼ avocado, sliced

¼ cup orange juice, freshly squeezed

1 garlic clove, crushed

2 tbsp extra virgin olive oil

1 tbsp yellow mustard

¼ tsp sea salt

¼ tsp black pepper

2 tbsp apple cider vinegar

¼ tbsp brown sugar

Preparation:

In a small bowl, whisk together orange juice, garlic clove, olive oil, mustard, salt, pepper, apple cider vinegar, and sugar. Mix well and set aside.

Rinse kale under cold running water and add to a deep pan.

Pour in enough water to cover and bring to a boil. Cook for 5 minutes.

Remove from the heat and drain. Transfer to a bowl along with pear, cranberries, and avocado. Mix well and sprinkle with the prepared dressing.

Serve.

Nutritional information per serving: Kcal: 269, Protein: 2.7g, Carbs: 24g, Fats: 19.4g

8. Garlic Eggplant Salad

Ingredients:

1 large eggplant, chopped into bite-sized pieces

4 large garlic cloves, chopped

½ cup walnuts, finely chopped

2 tbsp olive oil

1 tbsp apple cider vinegar

¼ cup cottage cheese

½ tsp smoked paprika

¼ tsp rosemary

Salt and pepper

Preparation:

Peel eggplant and cut into bite-sized pieces. Add to a medium sieve and generously sprinkle with salt. Let it sit for 15 minutes.

After about 15 minutes, rinse eggplant thoroughly under cold running water and drain. Set aside.

Grease a medium pan with olive oil and heat up to medium-high heat. Add garlic and cook for 1-2 minutes, stirring constantly.

Now, add drained eggplants and continue to cook for 15 minutes, stirring occasionally.

Meanwhile, in a small bowl, combine together apple cider vinegar, smoked paprika, rosemary, salt, and pepper.

Remove eggplants from the heat and trasnfer to a bowl. Add cottage cheese and walnuts. Sprinkle with apple cider mixture and stir well. Serve.

Nutritional information per serving: Kcal: 408, Protein: 14.1g, Carbs: 20.1g, Fats: 33.5g

9. Asparagus Salad with Dijon

Ingredients:

7oz asparagus, chopped into bite-sized pieces

1 small sweet potato, cut into chunks

1 tbsp dijon mustard

¼ cup plain Greek yogurt

1 tbsp parsley, finely chopped

½ tsp dried thyme

¼ tsp dried marjoram

2 tsp balsamic vinegar

1 tsp sugar

Salt and pepper to taste

Preparation:

Preheat a large grill pan over medium heat. Add asparagus and cook for 4-5 minutes, turning occasionally. Remove from the heat and cool for a while.

Meanwhile, rinse potato thoroughly under cold running water and rub the skin. Cut into bite-sized pieces and add to a deep pot. Pour in enough water to cover and bring to a boil. Cook until fork tender.

Remove potatoes from the heat and drain. Cool to a room temperature and transfer to a bowl along with asparagus.

In a small bowl, whisk togetehr dijon, Greek yogurt, parsley, thyme, marjoram, balsamic vinegar, sugar, salt, and pepper. Pour the mixture over salad and serve.

Nutritional information per serving: Kcal: 165, Protein: 12.2g, Carbs: 27.9g, Fats: 1.8g

10. Buckwheat and Lettuce Salad

Ingredients:

½ cup buckwheat groats

1 medium carrot, diced

1 cup lettuce, torn

2oz smoked salmon

2 tbsp olive oil

1 tbsp apple cider vinegar

Salt and pepper to taste

Preparation:

Add buckwheat to a small saucepan and pour in one cup of water. Sprinkle with some salt and bring to a boil over medium heat. Cook until buckwheat has absorbed all the liquid, about 12-15 minutes. When done, remove from the heat and drain. Cool to a room temperature. Transfer buckwheat to a bowl and add carrot, lettuce, and smoked salmon. Sprinkle with olive oil, apple cider vinegar, salt, and pepper.

Nutritional information per serving: Kcal: 543, Protein: 18.7g, Carbs: 50.1g, Fats: 32.4g

11. French Octopus Salad

Ingredients:

1 lb of fresh octopus

1 small onion, finely chopped

10 cherry tomatoes

¼ cup green olives

1 tbsp of capers

2 tbsp olive oil

2 tbsp freshly squeezed apple juice

1 tbsp of finely chopped parsley

Salt to taste

Preparation:

Place the octopus in a pressure cooker. Add 2 cups of water and seal the lid. Cook for about 40-45 minutes. Remove from the heat and allow it to cool for a while. Slice the octopus into bite-sized pieces and set aside.

Preheat two tablespoons of olive oil in a large skillet. Add the onions and stir-fry for five minutes. Now add apple juice, parsley, and octopus. Mix well and fry for about five more minutes. Remove from the heat and transfer to a bowl. Add halved cherry tomatoes, olives, and capers. Sprinkle with apple juice, parsley, and salt.

Keep it in the refrigerator for at least an hour before serving.

You can serve this salad with Swiss chard, or leeks.

Nutrition information per serving: Kcal: 328, Protein: 24.3g, Carbs: 11.3g, Fats: 21g

12. Orange Shrimp Salad

Ingredients:

1 lb large shrimps, peeled and deveined

2 tbsp freshly squeezed orange juice

1 tbsp cayenne pepper

1 tsp freshly ground black pepper

1 tsp pink Himalayan salt

4 garlic cloves, crushed

3 tbsp extra virgin olive oil

2 tablespoons fresh parsley, finely chopped

1 cup lettuce, chopped

1 large tomato, chopped

1 medium purple onion, diced

½ red bell pepper, sliced

Preparation:

In a large skillet, heat up the oil over medium-high heat. Add garlic and cook for 1 minute, stirring constantly. Now, throw in the shrimps and cook until nice golden color. Remove from the heat and cool for a while.

Meanwhile, wash and prepare the vegetables. Chop each piece and add to a bowl along with shrimps.

In a small bowl, whisk together orange juice, cayenne pepper, salt, black pepper, and parsley. Drizzle over salad and serve.

Nutrition information per serving: Kcal: 391, Protein: 43.6g, Carbs: 10.1g, Fats: 21.6g

13. Mussel and Arugula Salad

Ingredients:

10oz fresh mussels, debearded

1 medium onion, peeled and finely chopped

2 garlic cloves, crushed

1 tbsp fresh lemon juice

¼ cup fresh parsley, finely chopped

1 tbsp rosemary, finely chopped

1 cup lamb's lettuce, chopped

1 cup arugula leaves, chopped

1 cup cherry tomatoes, sliced

Sea salt to taste

Preparation:

Rinse and drain the mussels. Set aside.

Grease a non-stick frying pan with some cooking spray and heat over medium heat. Add onions and garlic. Cook until translucent.

Now, add mussels and continue to cook until crisp-tender.

Season with salt, pepper, and rosemary. Remove from the heat and cool for a while.

Meanwhile, wash and prepare vegetables. Add to a bowl along with mussels and mix all well.

Stir in parsley and lemon juice. Season with some more salt and pepper to taste and serve immediately.

Nutrition information per serving: Kcal: 358, Protein: 38.4g, Carbs: 34.1g, Fats: 7.7g

14. Spring Salad with Olives

Ingredients:

2 cups cherry tomatoes, sliced

1 cup black olives

1 medium onion, diced

2 radishes, sliced

A handful of lamb's lettuce

2 tbsp of freshly squeezed lime juice

3 tbsp of extra virgin olive oil

2 tbsp plain Greek yogurt

2 tbsp almonds, chopped

1 tbsp sesame seeds

1 tsp apple cider vinegar

Salt to taste

Preparation:

In a small bowl, whisk together olive oil, lime juice, Greek yogurt, chopped almonds, sesame seeds, apple cider vinegar, and salt. Set aside.

Slice each cherry tomato in half and add to a bowl along with olives, diced onions and sliced radishes.

Rinse lamb's lettuce thoroughly under cold running water and drain in a large sieve. Transfer to a bowl and mix well.

Drizzle with the almond mixture and toss to combine. Serve.

Nutrition information per serving: Kcal: 329, Protein: 3.4g, Carbs: 20.1g, Fats: 28.7g

15. Fresh Tomato Salad

Ingredients:

5-6 cherry tomatoes

1 medium onion, chopped

A handful of fresh lettuce, torn

½ cup fresh celery leaves, chopped

½ tsp dried oregano

½ tsp pink Himalayan salt

1 tbsp freshly squeezed lemon juice

Preparation:

Peel and finely chop onion. Place in a medium sieve and sprinkle with some salt. Let it sit for 10-12 minutes to remove the bitterness. When done, rinse well under cold running water and drain. Add to a bowl along with sliced cherry tomatoes. Wash lettuce and chop with your hands. Add to a bowl and mix well. Sprinkle with salt, oregano, and lemon juice before serving.

Nutrition information per serving: Kcal: 169, Protein: 7.2g, Carbs: 36.5g, Fats: 1.6g

16. Spinach Salad with Leeks

Ingredients:

12oz fresh spinach

3 large leeks, sliced

2 red onions, sliced

2 garlic cloves, crushed

2 tbsp goat's cheese

3 tbsp extra virgin olive oil

1 tsp sea salt

Preparation:

Heat up the olive oil over medium-high heat. Add sliced leek, garlic, and onions. Stir-fry for about five minutes, over medium heat.

Now add spinach and give it a good stir. Season with sea salt and continue to cook for 3 more minutes, stirring constantly.

Remove from the heat and sprinkle with fresh goat's cheese for some extra taste. However, keep in mind that even goat's cheese is slightly acidic. You have to limit the intake to maximum one tablespoon per serving.

Serve immediately.

Nutrition information per serving: Kcal: 301, Protein: 9.6g, Carbs: 24.7g, Fats: 20.4g

17. Chickpea Salad with Onions

Ingredients:

1 lb chickpeas, soaked

3 large purple onions, peeled and sliced

2 large tomatoes, roughly chopped

3 tbsp parsley, chopped

2 cups vegetable broth

1 tbsp cayenne pepper

2 tbsp olive oil

1 tsp salt

½ tsp freshly ground black pepper

Preparation:

Preheat the oil in a large saucepan over a medium-high heat. Add onions and saute for 4-5 minutes, or until translucent.

Now, add chickpeas, tomatoes, parsley, and vegetable broth.

Stir in cayenne pepper, salt, and freshly ground black pepper. Cover with a lid and bring it to a boil. Reduce the heat to low and cook for 25 minutes. Remove from the heat and cool to a room temperature.

Transfer to the refrigerator for at least an hour before serving.

Nutrition information per serving: Kcal: 513, Protein: 21.8g, Carbs: 68.3g, Fats: 19.1g

18. Greek Salad with Fresh Goat's Cheese

Ingredients:

5oz fresh goat's cheese

1 egg, boiled

1 cup red cabbage, shredded

Few lettuce leaves

1 medium tomato, chopped

1 small onion, sliced

½ cucumber, sliced

½ red bell pepper, sliced

Few olives

1 chili pepper, diced

2 tbsp cup olive oil

1 tsp mustard

1 tbsp finely chopped parsley

1 garlic clove, crushed

Sea salt to taste

Black pepper to taste

Preparation:

Gently place egg in a small pot and pour enough water to cover. Bring it to a boil and cook for 7 minutes. Remove from the heat and rinse under cold running water. Cool completely and peel. Transfer to a serving plate.

Wash and drain the vegetables. Cut and set aside.

Combine the olive oil with mustard, finely chopped parsley, and one garlic clove. Season with some salt and pepper and mix well.

Place the vegetables on a serving plate. Drizzle with the olive oil dressing and serve immediately.

Nutrition information per serving: Kcal: 283, Protein: 13.9g, Carbs: 11.7g, Fats: 21.3g

19. Halloumi Eggplant Salad

Ingredients:

2 medium eggplants, sliced in half

5oz halloumi cheese, sliced

2 large tomatoes, chopped

1 small cucumber, sliced

¼ cup fresh mint, chopped

¼ tsp dried marjoram

Salt to taste

For grilling:

2 tbsp olive oil

3 tbsp lemon juice, freshly squeezer

1 tsp red wine vinegar

½ tsp dried thyme

1 tbsp toasted sesame seeds

¼ tsp garlic powder

¼ tsp cumin powder

For dressing:

4 tbsp olive oil

1 small onion, diced

1 chili pepper, diced

¼ cup olives, sliced in half

3 tbsp pistachios, whole

1 tbsp lemon juice

Salt and pepper to taste

Preparation:

Slice eggplants lengthwise into ¼ inch thick slices. Generously sprinkle with salt and let it sit for 10 minutes. Rinse well the salt and drain. Pat dry with a piece of kitchen paper and set aside.

Slice halloumi into ½ inch thick slices. Set aside.

In a small bowl, whisk together all the ingredients for the grill – olive oil, lemon juice, red wine vinegar, thyme, sesame seeds, garlic powder, and cumin powder.

Brush eggplant and cheese with this mixture and set aside.

Preheat a large non-stick grill pan over medium-high heat. Add eggplant and cheese and grill until lightly golden brown. Remove from the pan and transfer to serving plate.

Meanwhile, combine all dressing ingredients in a small bowl. Pour the mixture over grilled eggplant and cheese.

Serve immediately.

Nutrition information per serving: Kcal: 457, Protein: 13.2g, Carbs: 27.8g, Fats: 35.9g

20. Quinoa Salad with Pomegranate Seeds

Ingredients:

½ cup quinoa

¼ cup buckwheat groats

1 blood orange, peeled

1 avocado, sliced

½ cup pomegranate seeds

1 cup baby spinach

½ cup cherry tomatoes, sliced

1 tbsp hazelnuts, chopped

1 tbsp sesame oil

Salt to taste

Preparation:

Add quinoa to a heavy-bottomed pot and pour in 1 ½ cup of water or vegetable stock. Bring to a boil over medium heat and cover with the lid. Reduce the heat to low and simmer for 15 minutes, stirring occasioanlly.

Remove quinoa from the heat and cool for a while. Set aside.

Meanwhile, place buckwheat in a small pot and pour in enough water to cover. Soak for 15-20 minutes. When done, transfer to a large sieve and drain.

Add cooked quinoa and soaked buckwheat groats to a bowl and mix well.

Now, rinse spinach under cold running water and add to a bowl along with the remaining vegetables. Add pomegranate seeds, hazelnuts, sliced avocado, and sesame oil. Sprinkle with some salt and serve.

Nutrition information per serving: Kcal: 378, Protein: 8.1g, Carbs: 44g, Fats: 20.8g

21. Creamy Rice Salad with Corn

Ingredients:

½ cup rice

1 tomato, chopped

¼ cup corn, drained

1 cup arugula, chopped

2oz feta, cubed

1 tbsp olive oil

Salt and pepper to taste

1 tbsp lemon juice

Preparation:

Add rice to a deep pot and pour in 1 ½ of water. Sprinkle with some salt and bring to a boil. Reduce the heat to medium-low and cook until all the water has evaporated. Stir occasionally. Remove from the heat and cool for a while. Transfer to a bowl and add tomato, corn, arugula, and feta. Sprinkle with olive oil, salt, pepper, lemon juice. Stir all well and serve.

Nutrition information per serving: Kcal: 328, Protein: 8.5g, Carbs: 43.4g, Fats: 13.7g

22. Sour Cabbage Salad

Ingredients:

2 cups cabbage, shredded

½ cup radishes, sliced

1 medium purple onion, diced

2 eggs, boiled

2 tbsp olive oil

2 tsp apple cider vinegar

1 tsp Italian seasoning

Preparation:

Add eggs to a pot of boiling water and sprinkle with salt. Cook for 10-12 minutes. When done remove from the heat and drain. Cool eggs completely and then gently peel.

Slice eggs and add to a bowl.

Meanwhile, sprinkle cabbage with salt and let it sit for 10 minutes. Rinse well and drain. Transfer to a bowl along with diced onion and sliced radishes.

Sprinkle with olive oil, apple cider vinegar, and Italian seasoning.

Toss well to combine and serve.

Nutrition information per serving: Kcal: 471, Protein: 14.5g, Carbs: 21.6g, Fats: 38.5g

23. Mediterranean Fusilli Salad

Ingredients:

2oz dry fussilli

10oz shrimp tails, peeled

1 cup cherry tomatoes, sliced

1 purple onion, diced

1 green chili pepper, diced

1 avocado, sliced

½ cup green olives, pits removed

½ cup fresh goat's cheese

1 tbsp olive oil

1 tsp apple cider vinegar

1 tsp Italian seasoning

Preparation:

Add fussilli to a deep pot and pour in enough water to cover. Sprinkle with some salt and bring to a boil. Mix well and cook pasta until al dente. Remove from the heat and drain. Transfer to a bowl and set aside.

Grease a large pan with olive oil and heat up over high heat.

Add shrimp tails and sprinkle with Italian seasoning. Cook for 3-4 minutes, turning once. Remove from the heat and add to a bowl with pasta.

Now, wash and prepare vegetables. Add to a bowl along with sliced avocado, olives, and goat's cheese. Sprinkle with apple cider vinegar and Italian seasoning.

Mix all well and serve.

Nutrition information per serving: Kcal: 387, Protein: 24.4g, Carbs: 27g, Fats: 21.3g

24. Baked Potato Salad with Onions

Ingredients:

1lb baby potatoes, whole

2oz smoked salmon

2 tbsp olive oil

2 large purple onions, sliced

2 garlic cloves, crushed

1 tbsp yellow mustard

1 tsp dried rosemary

Salt and pepper to taste

Preparation:

Preheat the oven to 350 degrees F. Line a baking sheet with parchment paper and set aside.

Rinse potatoes under cold running water and rub with salt. Add to the prepared baking sheet and sprinkle with rosemary. Bake for 40-45 minutes.

When done, remove from the oven and cool for a while.

Meanwhile, whisk together olive oil, crushed garlic, mustard, and some salt and pepper. Brush potatoes with this mixture and trasnfer to serving plate.

Add onions and smoked salmon. Serve.

Nutrition information per serving: Kcal: 356, Protein: 13.2g, Carbs: 44g, Fats: 16g

25. Couscous Salad

Ingredients:

1 cup couscous

2 medium tomatoes, sliced

1 cup lettuce, chopped

¼ cup fresh mint

1 medium onion, diced

1 tbsp almond butter

1 tbsp lemon juice

Salt and pepper to taste

1 tbsp olive oil

Preparation:

Add couscous to a deep, heavy-bottomed pot and pour in 1 ½ cup of water. Sprinkle with salt and bring to a boil. Reduce the heat to medium-low and cook for 10-15 minutes, or until couscous has absorbed all the liquid. Add almond butter and mix well. Remove from the heat and set aside.

Meanwhile, wash and prepare vegetables. Add to a bowl along with couscous. Mix well.

Sprinkle with lemon juice, olive oil, salt, and pepper. Serve.

Nutrition information per serving: Kcal: 489, Protein: 15g, Carbs: 80.4g, Fats: 12.6g

26. Chili Bean Salad

Ingredients:

1 cup kidney beans, drained

1 green bell pepper, sliced

3 red chili peppers, diced

2 tbsp pine nuts

1 tbsp macadamia nuts, chopped

1 medium purple onion

1 tbsp pumpkin seeds

2 tbsp olive oil

2 tbsp lemon juice

1 tsp garlic paste

1 tsp sweet chili sauce

Salt and pepper to taste

Preparation:

Add beans to a medium sieve and rinse thoroughly under cold running water. Drain and add to a bowl.

Wash the pepper and slice in half lengthwise. Remove stem and seeds. Rinse well and slice. Add to a bowl along with diced chili peppers.

Add pine nuts, sliced onions, macadamia nuts, and pumpkin seeds. Toss well to combine and set aside.

In a small bowl, whisk together olive oil, lemon juice, garlic paste, sweet chili sauce, some salt and pepper. Drizzle over salad and mix well.

Serve.

Nutrition information per serving: Kcal: 397, Protein: 16.5g, Carbs: 47.2g, Fats: 17.6g

27. Chickpea Cucumber Salad

Ingredients:

1 cup chickpeas, drained

1 jalapeno pepper, diced

1 tomato, chopped

1 cucumber, sliced

1 red bell pepper, sliced

1 onion, sliced

2 tbsp olive oil

2 tbsp lime juice

1 tbsp brown sugar

1 tsp garlic paste

¼ tsp cumin powder

Preparation:

Add chickpeas to a large sieve and rinse thoroughly under cold running water. Drain and add to a bowl along with chopped tomato, cucumber, bell pepper, and onion. Toss to combine and set aside.

Now, prepare the dressing. In a small bowl, combine

together olive oil, lime juice, brown sugar, garlic paste, and cumin powder. Mix well and optionally add one teaspoon of sesame seeds.

Drizzle over the vegetable mixture and refrigerate for about 30 minutes before serving.

Optionally, sprinkle with some more lemon juice before serving.

Nutrition information per serving: Kcal: 384, Protein: 14.7g, Carbs: 54.9g, Fats: 13.7g

28. Eggplant Salad with Nuts

Ingredients:

1 medium eggplant, sliced

1 cup cherry tomatoes, sliced

½ cup corn, drained

1 medium purple onion, diced

½ red bell pepper, sliced

1 small cucumber, sliced

¼ cup almonds, toasted

2 tbsp walnuts, minced

2 tbsp pine nuts

2 tbsp lemon juice

2 tbsp vegetable oil

1 tsp Worcestershire sauce

Salt and pepper to taste

Preparation:

Preheat the oven to 400 degrees F. Line a baking sheet with parchment paper and set aside.

Peel and slice eggplant. Arrange eggplant slices over the prepared baking sheet and sprinkle with salt. Bake for 20 minutes.

When done, remove from the oven and cool for a while. Transfer baked eggplant to serving plate and set aside.

Wash and prepare vegetables. Add to the plate along with nuts.

In a small bowl, mix together lemon juice, vegetable oil, Worcestershire sauce, salt, and pepper. Sprinkle over salad and serve.

Nutrition information per serving: Kcal: 462, Protein: 11.9g, Carbs: 42.3g, Fats: 31.5g

29. Creamy Beet Salad

Ingredients:

2 medium beets, sliced

2 eggs, boiled

1 cup plain Greek yogurt

½ cup sour cream

1 tbsp Dijon mustard

¼ cup parsley, finely chopped

3 garlic cloves, crushed

2 tbsp walnuts, finely chopped

2 tbsp almonds, finely chopped

1 cup arugula

1 tbsp grapeseed oil

Salt and pepper to taste

Preparation:

Add sliced beets to a deep pot and pour in enough water to cover. Generously sprinkle with salt and bring to a boil. Cook until fork-tender.

Remove beets from the heat and drain. Cool completely

and then transfer to serving bowl.

Meanwhile, add eggs to a pot of boiling water and cook for 12 minutes. Remove from the heat and drain. Cool for a while and peel. Slice eggs and add to a bowl with beets. Set aside.

In a medium bowl, mix together Greek yogurt, sour cream, dijon, parsley, and crushed garlic. Add walnuts and almonds. Mix well again and pour over beets and eggs.

Add arugula and sprinkle with oil, salt, and pepper. Toss to combine and serve.

Nutrition information per serving: Kcal: 470, Protein: 24.8g, Carbs: 22.1g, Fats: 32.9g

30. Caesar Salad with Cashews

Ingredients:

7oz chicken breast, boneless and skinless

½ cup croutons

1 cup lettuce, chopped

1 cup baby spinach, chopped

½ cucumber, sliced

2 eggs, boiled

½ tomato, sliced

2 tbsp plain Greek yogurt

2 tbsp sour cream

2oz cashews, chopped

1 tbsp lemon juice

Salt and pepper to taste

Preparation:

Preheat the oven to 400 degrees F. Line a baking pan with parchment paper and set aside.

Add eggs to a pot of boiling water and cook for 10 minutes. Remove from the heat and drain. Cool for a while and then peel. Set aside.

Rinse the meat thoroughly under cold running water and pat dry with a kitchen towel. Place on a large cutting board and cut into bite-sized pieces. Sprinkle with salt and pepper and add to the prepared baking pan. Bake for 20-25 minutes, or until golden brown.

Remove the meat from the oven and set aside.

Meanwhile, wash and prepare vegetables. Add to a bowl along with chilled meat, sliced eggs, and cashews.

Finally, combine Greek yogurt with sour cream, lemon juice, salt, and pepper. Pour the mixture over salad and serve.

Nutrition information per serving: Kcal: 429, Protein: 34.3g, Carbs: 21.6g, Fats: 23.5g

31. Lentil Salad

Ingredients:

1 cup cooked lentils

1 medium-sized red bell pepper

½ cup sweet corn

A handful of purple cabbage, shredded

A handful of lettuce, shredded

½ tsp salt

¼ tsp black pepper, freshly ground

2 tbsp olive oil

1 tbsp sesame seeds

Preparation:

First you have to cook your lentils. Use 3 cups of water for 1 cup of dry lentils. Cooked lentils will double in size. Keep this in mind when cooking. Bring the water to a boiling point, reduce the heat to medium and cover. Cook for about 15-20 minutes. Remove from the heat and drain. Transfer to a bowl.

Wash the pepper and cut lengthwise in half. Remove the seeds and stem. Chop into bite-sized pieces and set aside.

Combine cabbage and lettuce in a large colander. Rinse under running water and drain. Shred and set aside.

Now add other ingredients, season with salt, pepper, olive oil, and sprinkle with sesame seeds. Toss well to combine.

Nutrition information per serving: Kcal: 311, Protein: 11.6g, Carbs: 32.3g, Fats: 17.2g

32. Garlic Tuna with Asparagus and Avocado

Ingredients:

8oz fresh, wild asparagus

½ avocado, sliced

10oz tuna steak

2 garlic cloves

2 tbsp cooking oil

2 tbsp olive oil

Salt and freshly ground black pepper

¼ cup olives, sliced

Preparation:

Preheat the oil in a medium pan over medium heat. Season the tuna steak with some salt and pepper. Cook for 3-4 minutes on each side.

Remove from the pan and cool for a while. Flake the tuna steak into small pieces.

Clean and cut the asparagus into 2 inch long strips. Heat the remaining olive oil over a medium-high heat. Add asparagus and stir-fry for several minutes. Stir in garlic and mix well. Remove from the heat and use some kitchen paper to soak the excess oil.

Transfer to a serving platter and top with tuna. Add avocado and olives. Sprinkle with salt and pepper.

Serve.

Nutrition information per serving: Kcal: 385, Protein: 6.9g, Carbs: 9.7g, Fats: 37.7g

33. Crispy Beans with Lime Dressing

Ingredients:

½ red onion, sliced

1 cup green beans, cooked

3 cherry tomatoes, halved

½ red bell pepper, sliced

¼ cup of fresh lime juice

3 tbsp of olive oil

1 tsp of honey

½ small shallot, minced

1 garlic clove, crushed

¼ tsp of salt

Preparation:

In a small bowl, combine together olive oil and lime juice. Add honey, shallot, garlic, and salt. Whisk together until fully incorporated. Set aside.

Add the remaining ingredients in a serving bowl and drizzle with the prepared dressing. Toss well to combine and refrigerate for at least 30 minutes before serving.

Nutrition information per serving: Kcal: 265, Protein: 3.4g, Carbs: 19.7g, Fats: 21.6g

34. Chicken and Tofu Salad

Ingredients:

7oz chicken breast, boneless and skinless

¼ cup smoked tofu, sliced

1 cup lamb's lettuce

1 cup cherry tomatoes

½ cup button mushrooms, sliced

1 small zucchini, sliced

Salt and pepper to taste

2 tbsp olive oil

Preparation:

Wash and pat dry the meat with some kitchen paper. Cut into bite size pieces. Peel and chop zucchini.

Grease a large, non-stick grill pan with oil and heat over medium-high heat. Add the meat and cook for 7-10 minutes, stirring constantly. Remove the meat from the pan and add zucchini and mushrooms.

Continue to cook for another 10 minutes.

When done, remove from the heat and transfer to serving bowl. Add lamb's lettuce, tofu, and cherry toamtoes.

Sprinkle with olive oil, salt, and pepper. Toss well to combine and serve.

Nutrition information per serving: Kcal: 277, Protein: 24.5g, Carbs: 6.2g, Fats: 17.7g

35. Lettuce Salad with Walnuts

Ingredients:

2 cups lettuce, chopped

1 large orange, peeled

¼ cup walnuts

¼ cup dates, finely chopped

1 tbsp fresh lemon juice

Preparation:

Rinse the lettuce under cold running water and drain in a large colander. Gently squeeze with your hands and chop. Transfer to a serving bowl.

Add orange, walnuts, and dates. Sprinkle with lemon juice and toss well to combine.

Optionally, add a pinch of ground cumin and serve.

Nutrition information per serving: Kcal: 424, Protein: 11g, Carbs: 61.7g, Fats: 19.2g

36. Wild Salmon Salad with Lettuce and Fresh Lime

Ingredients:

10oz wild salmon fillets, skinless

7oz lettuce, torn

1 medium cucumber, sliced

2 eggs, boiled

½ cup sour cream

1 tbsp Dijon mustard

1 tbsp extra virgin olive oil

2 tbsp fresh lime juice

½ tsp salt

Preparation:

Preheat the oven to 425 degrees. Line a baking sheet with parchment paper and set aside.

Rinse the fillet and pat dry with a kitchen towel. Add to a cutting board and slice into 1-inch thick slices. Rub each with salt and transfer to the prepared baking sheet.

Bake for 15 minutes.

When done, remove from the oven and cool to a room

temperature. Set aside.

Meanwhile, wash and prepare the vegetables. Add to serving bowl and mix well.

Add eggs to a pot of boiling water and cook for 10 minutes. When done, remove from the heat and drain the water. Cool completely and then peel. Slice eggs and add to a bowl with vegetables. Set aside.

Finally, in a small bowl, whisk together sour cream, Dijon mustard, olive oil, lime juice, and salt. Brush the salmon with this mixture and serve over vegetables and eggs.

Nutrition information per serving: Kcal: 412, Protein: 39.1g, Carbs: 11.7g, Fats: 25.3g

37. Leek Salad with Avocado and Salmon

Ingredients:

2 leeks, chopped into bite-sized pieces

7oz salmon fillet, skinless

½ avocado, sliced

1 tsp dried thyme

½ tsp dried rosemary

2 tbsp olive oil

Salt and freshly ground black pepper

Preparation:

Grease a medium skillet with olive oil and heat over high heat. Clean and wash leeks. Cut into bite-sized pieces and add to the skillet. Cook for 8-10 minutes, stirring constantly.

When done, remove leeks from the skillet and transfer to serving bowl.

Now, rub the salmon fillet with salt and pepper and add to the pan. Cook for 5-6 minutes on each side.

When done, remove from the heat and add to serving bowl along with sliced avocado. Sprinkle with some more salt and pepper, dried thyme, and rosemary.

Toss well to combine and serve.

Nutrition information per serving: Kcal: 410, Protein: 21.6g, Carbs: 17.4g, Fats: 30.3g

38. Fresh Vegetables with Cubed Tofu

Ingredients:

8oz smoked tofu, cubed

1 large tomato, sliced

1 cup baby spinach, chopped

1 small onion, diced

1 small carrot, diced

1 green chili, diced

1 tbsp butter

1 tsp soy sauce

2 tsp oyster sauce

½ tsp garlic powder

Salt and pepper to taste

Preparation:

Melt the butter in a small pan over medium heat. Add cubed tofu and sprinkle with salt and pepper. Cook for 2-3 minutes and then add soy sauce, oyster sauce, and garlic powder. Continue to cook for another 2 minutes. Remove from the heat and transfer to a bowl.

Meanwhile, wash and prepare vegetables. Add to a bowl and mix well to combine. Optionally, season with some more salt or pepper to taste and sprinkle with some freshly squeezed lemon juice.

Serve.

Nutrition information per serving: Kcal: 309, Protein: 23.5g, Carbs: 14.4g, Fats: 18.2g

39. Spicy Avocado Salad

Ingredients

1 ripe avocado, sliced

2 red chili peppers, diced

2 cups baby spinach

1 cup arugula, chopped

1 onion, diced

2 tbsp sesame oil

1 tsp sriracha

1 tbsp soy sauce

1 tsp mirin

½ tsp garlic powder

Preparation:

Preheat a large wok pan over high heat. Sprinkle with pan with sesame oil and add sliced avocado. Cook for 2 minutes on high heat and then sprinkle with soy sauce, sriracha, mirin, and garlic powder. Continue to cook for another 2-3 minutes, stirring constantly.

Remove from the heat and transfer to bowl. Set aside.

Now, rinse and prepare the vegetables. Add to serving bowl and mix with avocado. Optionally, season with some salt or sprinkle with lime juice.

Serve.

Nutrition information per serving: Kcal: 371, Protein: 4.3g, Carbs: 18.4g, Fats: 33.5g

40. Zesty Quinoa Salad

Ingredients:

1 cup quinoa, dry

1 medium carrot, grated

1 cup green peas, drained

2 tbsp lemon juice

1 tbsp orange juice

Zest of one lemon

½ tsp garlic powder

2 tbsp olive oil

Preparation:

Add quinoa to a heavy-bottomed pot and pour in two cups of water. Sprinkle with some salt and garlic powder. Bring to a boil and reduce the heat to low. Stir well and cook until all the liquid has evaporated. Remove from the heat and transfer to a bowl.

Add grated carrot and green peas. Stir in lemon juice, orange juice, and lemon zest. Sprinkle salad with olive oil and toss to combine.

Serve immediately.

Nutrition information per serving: Kcal: 342, Protein: 11g, Carbs: 46.4g, Fats: 13g

41. Black Bean Salad with Cheese and Mushrooms

Ingredients:

1 cup black beans, drained

½ cup green peas

2 spring onions, chopped

1 cup sliced shiitake mushrooms

¼ cup cottage cheese

½ cup plain Greek yogurt

2 boiled eggs, sliced

1 tbsp olive oil

Salt and pepper to taste

Preparation:

Grease a non-stick fryin pan with olive oil and heat over medium-high heat. Add spring onions and sprinkle with salt. Cook for 3-4 minutes, stirring constantly.

Now, add shiitake mushrooms and season with some more salt and pepper. Continue to cook for 7-8 minutes, stirring constantly. Remove from the heat and set aside.

Meanwhile, boil eggs for 10 minutes. Remove from the heat and drain. Cool for a while and peeel. Transfer to a owl along with drained black beans and green peas. Add the shiiteke mixture and stir in cottage cheese. Mix all well.

Pour the Greek yogurt over salad and sprinkle with olive oil, salt, and pepper. Serve.

Nutrition information per serving: Kcal: 397, Protein: 24.6g, Carbs: 55g, Fats: 9.6g

42. Herring and Romaine Lettuce Salad

Ingredients:

7oz herring fillets, canned

1 cucumber, sliced

1 carrot, finely chopped

3 olives

1 cup romaine lettuce, torn

2 tbsp olive oil

2 tbsp lemon juice

1 tbsp dill, finely chopped

Salt and pepper to taste

½ tsp chili powder

Preparation:

Peel and thinly slice cucumber. Set aside.

Using a colander, rinse the lettuce under running water. Drain and set aside.

Now, combine cucumber, carrto and lettuce on a serving plate.

Drain herring fillets and add to serving plate. Sprinkle with salt, pepper, dill, chili powder, and olive oil. Mix well to combine and top with olives.

Refrigerate for 30 minutes before serving.

Nutrition information per serving: Kcal: 375, Protein: 24.7g, Carbs: 10.9g, Fats: 26.6g

43. Chicken Cucumber Salad

Ingredients:

7oz chicken breast, boneless and skinless

1 cucumber, sliced

1 red pepper, sliced

2 slices bread, lightly toasted

1 tomato, chopped

1 cup lettuce, chopped

2 tsp taco seasoning

2 tbsp honey

2 tbsp olive oil

2 tbsp lemon juice

½ tsp dried celery

Salt and pepper to taste

Preparation:

Preheat the oven to 350 degrees. Line a baking sheet with parchment paper and set aside.

Rinse the meat and pat dry with a kitchen towel. Cut into bite-sized pieces and add to the prepared baking sheet.

Sprinkle with salt and bake for 30 minutes.

When done, remove from the oven and transfer to a bowl along with cucumber, red pepper, bread, tomato, and lettuce. Mix well and set aside.

In a small bowl, whisk together raco seasoning, honey, olive oil, lemon juice, celery, salt, and pepper. Drizzle over salad and toss to combine.

Serve.

Nutrition information per serving: Kcal: 381, Protein: 23.9g, Carbs: 35.2g, Fats: 17.3g

44. Lemon Shrimp Salad

Ingredients:

7oz cleaned shrimps

1 cup lettuce mix

½ sliced purple onion

1 chopped tomato

1 sliced carrot

½ cup chopped arugula

1 tbsp olive oil

1 tbsp lemon juice

1 tsp lemon zest

½ tsp salt

¼ tsp dried thyme

¼ tsp fresh rosemary

¼ cup white wine

Preparation:

Rinse shrimps under cold running water and drain in a large sieve. Grease a non-stick skillet with olive oil and heat up over medium-high heat. Add shrimps and season with salt, dried thyme, and rosemary. Briefly cook for 3-4 minutes, stirring constantly.

Now, pour in the wine and give it a good stir. Continue to cook for 5 minutes.

Remove from the heat and set aside. In a large bowl, combine together lettuce, sliced onion, tomato, carrot, and arugula. Add shrimps and sprinkle with lemon juice and lemon zest. If necessary, season with some more salt or dried herbs.

Serve immediately.

Nutritional information per serving: Kcal: 483, Protein: 48.6g, Carbs: 22g, Fats: 18g

45. Thai Salmon Salad

Ingredients:

4oz thinly sliced salmon fillets

¼ cup sliced cucumber

2 tbsp fresh lime juice

1 tbsp sweet chili sauce

1 tsp brown sugar

1 sliced red chili pepper

1 tsp chopped Thai basil

1 1-inch grated ginger knob

2 tsp finely chopped peanuts

a few lettuce leaves for serving

Preparation:

In a small bowl, combine lime juice, sweet chili sauce, peanuts, and sugar. Stir to combine and then add salmon fillets. Mix to coat well and let it marinate for 20 minutes.

Meanwhile, prepare the salad. Combine cucumber, chili pepper, basil, and basil on a sheet of lettuce leaves.

Use half of the previously prepared marinade and drizzle

over the salad.

Now, preheat the avocado oil in a small saucepan over a medium-high heat. Add salmon and cook for 2-3 minutes on each side. Top the salad with salmon and drizzle with the remaining marinade.

Sprinkle all with fresh ginger and serve immediately.

Nutritional information per serving: Kcal: 456, Protein: 35.7g, Carbs: 16g, Fats: 29.1g

46. Cold Chicken and Broccoli Salad with Rice

Ingredients:

3oz chicken breast

1 cup chopped broccoli

1 sliced red bell pepper

¼ cup rice

2 tbsp soy sauce

2 tsp sesame oil

1 tbsp rice vinegar

½ tsp chili powder

1 tsp sugar

¼ tsp white pepper

Salt to taste

Preparation:

Rinse the chicken under cold running water and pat dry with some kitchen paper. Place on a large cutting board and cut into bite-sized pieces. Set aside.

Grease a large wok pan with sesame oil and heat up over high heat. Add chopped chicken and cook for 4-5 minutes, stirring constantly. Now add bell pepper and broccoli. Drizzle with soy sauce and rice vinegar and sprinkle with chili powder, sugar, salt, and freshly ground white pepper.

Continue to cook until broccoli has completely softened.

Remove from the heat and set aside.

Prepare the rice according to package instructions or place in a small saucepan and pour in 3/4 cup of water. Sprinkle with some salt and bring it to a boil. Reduce the heat to low and cook until all the liquid has evaporated.

Serve with the chicken mixture.

Nutritional information per serving: Kcal: 457, Protein: 27.3g, Carbs: 58g, Fats: 12.1g

47. Baked Chicken Salad

Ingredients:

10oz chicken breast

1 cup arugula

1 cup cherry tomatoes

1 cup baby spinach

2 tsp olive oil

1 tbsp lemon juice

½ tsp chili powder

1 tbsp soy sauce

Salt and pepper to taste

Preparation:

Preheat the oven to 350 degrees F. Line a baking sheet with some parchment paper and set aside.

In a small bowl, whisk together olive oil, soy sauce, lemon juice, chili powder, and soy sauce. Season with salt and pepper to taste and set aside.

Rinse well the meat and generously brush with the prepared mixture. Bake for 25-30 minutes.

When done, remove from the oven and cool for a while. Transfer to a cutting board and cut into approximately 1/4-inch thick slices. Place in a bowl along with the remaining ingredients and optionally season with some more salt or sprinkle with lemon juice.

Toss to combine and serve.

Nutritional information per serving: Kcal: 464, Protein: 64.4g, Carbs: 11g, Fats: 17g

48. Shrip Taco Cole Slaw Salad

Ingredients:

2 taco shells

3oz peeled and deveined shrimps

2 sliced cherry tomatoes

1 cup shredded cabbage

½ grated carrot

2 tbsp sour cream

2 tbsp Greek yogurt

2 tsp white vinegar

1 tsp dry mustard

1 tsp dried celery

salt and pepper to taste

lemon juice to taste

Preparation:

Prepare taco shells according to package directions and set aside.

In a large bowl, combine together cabbage and carrot. Add sour cream, Greek yogurt, mustard, vinegar, celery, salt and pepper to taste. Toss well to combine and set aside.

Preheat a non-stick grill pan or an electric grill to high heat. Grill shrimps for 3-4 minutes. Stuff each taco shell with the cabbage mixture, add tomatoes, and top with grilled shrimps.

Drizzle with freshly squeezed lime juice and serve immediately.

Nutritional information per serving: Kcal: 448, Protein: 28.2g, Carbs: 45g, Fats: 18.3g

49. Quinoa with Salmon and Beans

Ingredients:

¼ cup quinoa

¼ cup black beans

3oz salmon fillet

1 chopped tomato

2 tbsp drained corn

1 tsp ground dried shiitake

½ tsp salt

¼ tsp dried thyme

1 tbsp lemon juice

1 tbsp finely chopped parsley

Preparation:

Place quinoa in a small saucepan and pour in 1/2 cup of water. Sprinkle with some salt and bring to a boil. Reduce the heat to medium-low and simmer until all the liquid has evaporated. Stir occasionally.

Remove from the heat and set aside.

Grease a non-stick frying pan with some cooking spray and

heat up over medium-high heat. Rinse fillets under cold running water and place on a cutting board. Using a sharp knife, cut into bite-sized pieces and transfer to the frying pan.

Cook for 3-4 minutes, stirring constantly. Stir in chopped tomato and pour in about 1/4 cup of water. Continue to cook for 5 minutes.

Finally, stir in cooked quinoa, corn, and black beans. Season with salt, thyme, and ground shiitake. Stir all well and remove from the heat.

Sprinkle with fresh parsley and lemon juice before serving.

Nutritional information per serving: Kcal: 464, Protein: 34.7g, Carbs: 63g, Fats: 9.7g

50. Creamy Chicken Salad with Cheese

Ingredients:

7oz chicken breast

1 cup cherry tomatoes

1 cup arugula

1 cup lettuce

½ sliced purple onion

2 tbsp feta cheese

½ tsp dried chives

¼ tsp dried oregano

½ tsp salt

1 tbsp lemon juice

1 tbsp olive oil

Preparation:

Preheat a non-stick grill pan or an electric grill to high heat.

Rinse the meat under cold running water and rub with salt, chives, and oregano. Grill for 4-5 minutes on each side and remove from the heat.

Transfer to a bowl and add vegetables. Sprinkle with olive

oil, lemon juice and top with cheese.

Serve immediately.

Nutritional information per serving: Kcal: 468, Protein: 48g, Carbs: 16.8g, Fats: 24g

MEAL RECIPES

1. Collard Green Surprise

Ingredients:

¼ cup extra virgin olive oil

1 16 oz. bag collard greens

2 cloves garlic

¼ teaspoon red pepper flakes

Pinch of salt

How to Prepare:

Boil collard greens in a pot of salted water for 5 minutes, then strain. Heat olive oil and garlic in a sauté pan. When the garlic starts to cook add the collard greens, salt and pepper flakes. Sauté till well coated and the greens begin to fry in the oil. Serve warm or cold.

2.   Super Green Eggs

Ingredients:

6 eggs

½ cup milk

¼ cup sour cream

¼ cup extra virgin olive oil

1 small onion

¼ cup cheese of choice

1 16 oz. bag collard greens

¼ teaspoons red pepper flakes

Pinch of salt

How to Prepare:

Beat the eggs, salt and pepper, milk and sour cream in a bow. Sauté thinly chopped onions in a skillet with one tablespoon of olive oil. Add the egg mixture and let cook slowly until the eggs are almost firm. Add the collard greens, cheese, and the pepper flakes. Fold the eggs over the collard greens and cook until the greens are soft and the eggs are firm.

3. Painted Beans and Greens

Ingredients:

1 can precooked pinto beans

1 16 oz. bag of collard greens

1 cup chicken stock

Pinch salt and pepper

1 tbsp. red pepper flakes

1 tbsp. olive oil

1 clove garlic

1 tsp. chili powder

How to Prepare:

Boil a pot of salted water and add the collard greens, boil till soft. Drain. In a skillet sauté garlic and oil. Add onions and cook until mixture is clear.

Add the chicken stock and add the pinto beans that have been rinsed and drained. Heat thoroughly and add the drained collard greens. Add the chili powder, salt pepper, and pepper flakes. Cook until the collards are soft.

This dish is also good served the next day after the flavors have blended.

4. Collard Green Salad

Ingredients:

1 16 oz. bag collard greens

1 bag mixed salad vegetables

1 tomato diced

1 red pepper diced

1 cucumber

1 red onion

3 tbsp. Herb flavored Olive oil (olive oil infused with rosemary and basil especially)

2 tbsp. Red Wine vinegar

Salt and Pepper to taste.

How to Prepare:

Combine all ingredients in a large bowl and mix.

Eat chilled.

5. Green Toast

Ingredients:

1 Loaf Italian Bread

1 tbsp. olive oil

1 clove garlic

1 tsp. parsley

1 tsp. basil

1 tsp. oregano

Pinch of salt and pepper

1 bag collard greens cooked and drained

1 lb. shredded mozzarella cheese

How to Prepare:

Slice Bread lengthwise. Using a pestle mash the spices and garlic with the olive oil until paste is formed. Spread the paste on the bread.

Strain the collard greens in your hands and dry with a towel. Remove as much moisture as possible. Layer the collard greens over the paste.

Add the mozzarella on top and broil until the cheese melts. Eat warm

6. Green Pasta

Ingredients:

3 eggs

3 cups flour

1 cup water

1 tsp. salt

8 oz. collard greens cooked and drained.

How to Prepare:

Drain the collard greens after boiling until all the water is out of them.

In a mixer add eggs, water and salt. Slowly add the flour while mixing constantly on a low speed. When the dough comes together it is time to add the collard greens. Incorporate them thoroughly into the dough.

Let the dough sit for about 20 minutes covered with a damp cloth.

Using a pasta machine work the dough through the machine until the desired shape appears. Dry until ready to cook.

7. Green Pasta with Lemon Pepper Sauce

Ingredients:

Green Pasta

3 Lemons (One sliced into thin slices, two juiced)

1 tsp. black pepper

1 garlic glove

2 tsp. olive oil

¼ cup parmesan Cheese, Grated

How to Prepare:

Cook pasta in a large pot with salted water. Dry pasta should take about 6 minutes for an 'al dente' texture.

To prepare the sauce, sauté the garlic in the olive oil. Slowly add the juice of 2 lemons and the slices of one lemon. Add the salt and black pepper. Add 1 tablespoon of the grated cheese.

Add the al dente pasta to the skillet and add some the pasta water to combine as a sauce.

Add more parmesan cheese to your preference.

8. Green Soup

Ingredients:

1-quart chicken stock

1 16 oz. bag collard greens

1 cup cubed bread pieces

1 12 oz. bag of shredded carrots

1 small onion, minced

1 tbsp. minced garlic

1 tbsp. olive oil

¼ cup mushrooms, washed, sliced

How to Prepare:

Boil and drain collard green in a pan of salted water. Drain.

In a soup pan, add olive oil and sauté minced garlic, minced onion, and sliced mushrooms. Add the carrots and collard greens.

Add the stock to the pan and heat through. Add the cubed bread and serve.

9. Green Grilled Chicken Breast

Ingredients:

4 skinless chicken breasts

8 oz. collard greens boiled and drained

1 garlic clove, minced

1 tbsp. olive oil

2 slices mozzarella cheese

2 slices roasted red peppers

1 tsp. crushed red pepper flakes

Salt and paper to taste

How to Prepare:

Grill chicken breast until just about cooked. Remove from grill.

In a sauté pan add the minced garlic in the olive oil and add the drained collard greens. Add the pepper flakes. Remove from pan.

Transfer the chicken to the skillet and add the salt and pepper. Layer the collard greens, roasted red peppers and top with cheese. Cook until the cheese is melted and the wellness is to your liking.

10. Green Rice

Ingredients:

2 cups cooked wild rice

1 16 oz. bag of collard greens cooked and chopped

1-cup chicken stock

3 slices turkey bacon, chopped

1 can black beans, precooked

1 small onion chopped

1 glove garlic chopped

1 tbsp. olive oil

Salt and pepper to taste

How to Prepare:

Sauté turkey bacon, olive oil, garlic and onion. Add chicken stock. Season with salt and pepper and transfer to a large pan. To this large pan, add the precooked beans and cooked wild rice. Heat for 5 minutes, while stirring well. Add salt and pepper to taste, then serve.

11. Red and Green Salad

Ingredients:

1 bunch Broccoli stem cut off

1-cup cherry tomatoes

2 cups cooked tortellini

1 small can sliced black olives

1 small red onion

1 tbsp. olive oil

1 tsp. red wine vinegar

1 tsp. oregano

Pinch of salt and pepper

How to Prepare:

Blanch broccoli crowns, cut cherry tomatoes in half, drain olives, and chop the red onion.

Add the cooked tortellini and all ingredients in a large bowl. Toss with oil, vinegar and oregano. Add salt and pepper to taste. Chill before serving.

12. Broccoli Soup

Ingredients:

1 cup chicken stock

1 bunch broccoli stems removed

1 glove garlic, minced

1-cup heavy cream

½ cup cheddar cheese

1 small onion chopped

Pinch of salt and pepper

How to Prepare:

In a soup pan, sauté onion and garlic. Add the broccoli florets and continue to cook until the broccoli is soft. Add salt and pepper.

Add the chicken stock and boil at low heat. Add heavy cream and slowly warm the soup to high heat for 4 minutes. Add the cheddar cheese and slowly bring back to a low heat. Allow to cool, then serve at desired temperature.

13. Chicken, Rice and Broccoli

Ingredients:

2 cups cooked wild rice

2 chicken breast cubed

1 tbsp. Olive oil

1 Garlic clove, minced

1 broccoli crown

1 lemon, sliced

Pinch of salt and pepper

How to Prepare:

Clean broccoli crown and chop until the pieces are uniform. In a steamer add the broccoli and sliced lemon into the water. Steam for five minutes or until the desired level of softness of the broccoli.

Saute the olive oil with garlic in a pan and add the chicken cubes. Add the pinch of salt and pepper to taste. Cook for about 10 minutes until chicken shows no sign of pink and is completely white in the center of the cubes.

Add the broccoli crowns and toss with the chicken cubes.

In large bowl, pour over the wild rice, then serve.

14. Chicken and Broccoli

Ingredients:

4 chicken thighs

1 broccoli crown cut into florets

2 large russet potatoes, washed.

Salt and paper to taste

6 chipotle onions, minced

1 tsp. olive oil

How to Prepare:

Sauté the thighs to crisp the crust. Add to the baking pan with potatoes sliced into ¼ inch slices, and minced chipotle onions. Add salt and Pepper to taste. Add olive oil and the remaining oil from the sauté pan. After 30 minutes in a 350 degree F oven, add the broccoli and toss to blend. Finish cooking until the chicken is cooked completely and the potatoes are soft, then serve.

15. Broccoli Cheese cakes

Ingredients:

1 crown of broccoli

½ cup grated Parmesan cheese

2 eggs

1 tsp. salt

1 cup flavored breadcrumbs

1 tbsp. olive oil

How to Prepare:

Steam broccoli florets in a water and lemon steamer. Allow to cool, then pulse in a mixer until the consistency of large breadcrumbs. Add eggs, cheese, salt and pulse again. When mixed add the breadcrumbs. Heat the olive oil in a skillet. With an ice cream scooper, scoop out a portion of the broccoli/breadcrumb mix and flatten on the skillet. Fry until crispy on the one side and then flip. Fry on the other side until crispy. Serve with your favorite dipping sauce.

16. Broccoli Chicken Farfalle

Ingredients:

1 lb. farfalle pasta

1 broccoli floret

2 cups cooked chicken, squared

2 garlic cloves, crushed

2 tbsp. red pepper flakes

2 tbsp. olive oil

Salt and pepper to taste

Grated Cheese

How to Prepare:

While the salted pasta water is boiling, sauté the crushed garlic clove in olive oil in a frying pan. Add the broccoli floret and the squared, cooked chicken to the sauté and cook for 2 minutes, then set aside.

Cook the farfalle pasta until desired texture, then drain. Then combine the pasta, broccoli, and chicken together and mix. Top with the grated cheese and red pepper flakes, then serve.

17. Broccoli Muffins

Ingredients:

1 broccoli crown chopped fine

1 onion chopped fine

½ cup chopped carrots

6 eggs

½ cup cheddar cheese, shredded

2 cups flour

2 tsp. baking powder

1 tbsp. sugar

1 tsp. salt

How to Prepare:

In a large bowl beat the eggs. Add the vegetables and mix thoroughly. Add the shredded cheddar cheese, flour, baking powder, sugar and salt, and mix well.

Scoop into muffin cup baking tins.

Bake at 350 degrees F for 30 minutes.

Allow to cool and then serve.

18. Roasted Broccoli

Ingredients:

1 crown broccoli cut into florets

1 lemon, juiced

Pinch of salt and pepper

Pinch garlic powder

½ tsp. Chili powder

1-tbsp. olive oil

How to Prepare:

Preheat oven to 400 degrees. In a large bowl, toss broccoli florets with olive oil, garlic powder, salt, pepper and chili powder.

Place tossed broccoli florets on a baking pan and roast for 5 minutes. Then turn and finish roasting for another 3 minutes.

Remove from the oven, and allow to cool. Toss with the lemon juice, then serve.

19. Honey Orange Chicken

Ingredients:

2 chicken breast, cubed and dusted with flour

1 orange, juiced

1 tbsp. olive oil

½ cup honey

1 tbsp. sesame seeds

2 cups cooked rice of your choice

Pinch of salt and pepper

How to Prepare::

Sauté chicken cubes in olive oil to get a dark brown coating on the cubes. Transfer to a baking pan.

In a small bowl, mix the orange juice and honey. Add sesame seeds, then drizzle over chicken cubes.

Bake covered for 20 minutes at 350 degrees F or until the cubes are white and done in the center. Add salt and pepper to taste.

Serve over cooked rice of your choice.

20. Buffalo Style Cod Fish

Ingredients:

4 cod filets coated with cornmeal

¼ cup hot sauce

¼ cup warmed olive oil

Pinch of salt and pepper to taste

How to Prepare:

Warm the olive oil and hot sauce together in a saucepan.

Dip the coated cod filets in the mixture and place on a baking sheet.

Brush remaining mixture to fully coat the filets.

Bake covered for 10 minutes at 350 degrees F. Serve with sides of choice, such as celery and carrot sticks with bleu cheese dressing.

21. Squash and Beet salad

Ingredients:

1-cup butternut squash roasted

1-cup beets roasted

1 green apple, chopped

½ cup pecans

2 cups arugula

1 cup orange sections

1 orange, juiced

How to Prepare:

Toss the arugula, green apple, squash, beets and pecans in a bowl. Add the orange sections. Dress with the orange juice. Chill to allow the flavors to infuse each other.

22. Orange Sections salad

Ingredients:

1 cup orange sections

1 sliced red onion

2 cups salad greens of choice

½ cup shredded carrots

1 cup sliced tomatoes

1 tbsp. olive oil

½ tbsp. balsamic vinegar

Salt and pepper to taste

How to Prepare:

In a large salad bowl, mix the salad greens, orange sections, onion slices, shredded carrots, and sliced tomatoes. Let them rest for a few minutes. In a small bowl, mix the olive oil and balsamic vinegar together, then toss over the salad, and serve cold preferably.

23. Orange Rice

Ingredients:

2 cups rice cooked of your choice

1 small onion chopped

1 small pepper chopped

1-cup broccoli in small pieces

½ cup shredded carrots

1 orange, juiced

½ tbsp. olive oil

Pinch of salt and pepper

How to Prepare:

Heat olive oil in a saucepan and add onions. Cook till onions are clear. Add broccoli, pepper, carrots and cook until tender. Add orange juice and heat for 1 minute. Add salt and pepper. Add rice to the saucepan and stir till well blended. Keep covered and cook on low heat for 5 minutes.

Serve warm. You may add a protein such as cooked chicken or cod, as your prefer.

24. Chicken a la orange

Ingredients:

1 roasting chicken with the inners removed and washed.

1 whole garlic glove

4 oranges, juiced

1 spring rosemary

3 basil leaves

1 tbsp. olive oil

Pinch of salt and pepper

How to Prepare:

In a crock-pot place half of the orange juice. Place the whole garlic glove, spring rosemary, and basil leaves in the cavity of the chicken. Place the chicken in the crock pot and add the salt and pepper. Pour the olive oil. Pinch small holes in the chicken and pour the other half of the orange juice over the top of the chicken. Let cook for six hours, then serve.

25. Citrus Lobster Salad

Ingredients:

1 cup of lobster meat. This can be frozen or removed from a fresh steamed lobster

1-cup orange slices

1 small red onion chopped

½ cup shredded carrots

1-cup arugula

2 tbsp. lemon juice

1 tsp. horseradish

2 tbsp. olive oil

How to Prepare:

In a large salad bowl, mix the arugula, orange slices, shredded carrots, and chopped onions. Add lobster meat on top of salad mixture.

Dress the salad lightly with olive oil, lemon juice and dot with horseradish, then serve.

26. Eggs and Avocado and Tuna

Ingredients:

3 hard-boiled eggs

1 avocado

Pinch of salt and pepper

1 can tuna in oil

How to Prepare:

Clean boiled eggs and chop. Clean out avocado and cut into bite size pieces. In a medium bowl, mix the chopped eggs with the avocado and add the tuna with the oil from the can. Mix lightly, adding the salt and pepper, then serve.

27. French Toast Bake

Ingredients:

8 eggs

½ cup milk

1 loaf of bread of your choice

1 tbsp. olive oil

½ cup maple syrup

1 tsp. vanilla extract

How to Prepare:

The night before soak the loaf of bread in milk and let it rest in the refrigerator overnight. When ready to prepare, place the soaked bread on a baking pan. In a medium bowl, beat the eggs with ½ cup of milk, add the vanilla extract and olive oil, and pour on top of loaf of bread to cover completely.

Bake at 350 degrees F for 10 minutes then remove from oven. Serve warm with maple syrup.

28. Egg Bake

Ingredients:

8 eggs

1-cup milk

1 pinch salt and pepper

1 package hash browns

1 package turkey sausage, precooked

1 small green pepper, chopped

½ cup cheddar cheese, shredded

How to Prepare:

In a baking pan, layer the sausage on the bottom, then layer the hash browns on top of the sausage.

In a medium bowl, beat the eggs, add milk, salt and pepper, peppers, and the shredded cheddar cheese. Pour onto the pan over the potatoes and allow seeping in between the potatoes. Bake for 10 minutes

This can be left overnight in the refrigerator and baked the next day or it can be baked at this point.

29. Italian Cod

Ingredients:

4 cod filets

2 boiled russet potatoes, peeled

1-cup green beans steamed

1 small red onion chopped

1 small red pepper chopped

1 clove garlic chopped

Pinch of salt and pepper

2 tbsp. olive oil

1 tbsp. red wine vinegar

How to Prepare:

Sauté the codfish in a frying pan with olive oil until it flakes apart. Slice the codfish filets into small flakes.

Dice the peeled, boiled potatoes into medium size cubes. Steam green beans to the crispness that you prefer, then allow to cool. In a large bowl, mix the green beans, potato cubes, onions, chopped peppers and chopped garlic.

Add the cod filets flakes and toss with olive oil and vinegar.

Serve warm or cold.

30. Egg Soup

Ingredients:

2 cups chicken stock

2 eggs

½ cup Parmesan cheese

½ cup shredded carrots

¼ tsp. garlic powder

¼ tsp. salt and pepper

How to Prepare:

Heat chicken stock with shredded carrots until it boils. Add salt and pepper.

In a small bowl, beat the eggs and add to the boiling chicken stock while stirring. Boil for 2 minutes, then add Parmesan cheese. Remove from heat and serve at desired temperature.

31. Egg Salad Stuffed Tomatoes

Ingredients:

6 hard-boiled eggs, chopped

1 avocado chopped in small pieces

½ cup sour cream

1 chopped onion

½ cup chopped celery

½ cup chopped carrots

1 lime, juiced

4 medium size tomatoes cored

How to Prepare:

In a medium bowl mix the chopped eggs with the chopped onion, carrots and celery. Then add the avocado pieces and pour the lime juice into the bowl. Dress with sour cream, then stuff each of the tomatoes with the filling and enjoy. May add salt and pepper to your taste.

32.   Frittatas

Ingredients:

8 eggs

½ cup milk

1 small onion chopped

1-cup mozzarella cheese, grated

½ cup mushrooms sliced

½ cup red pepper strips

1 baked potato

2 tbsp. olive oil

¼ cup parmesan cheese

How to Prepare:

In a large mixing bowl whisk the eggs, add a dash of salt and pepper and Parmesan cheese.

In a large saucepan with olive oil, add the onions and sauté. Add the mushrooms, red pepper strips and sauté till slightly tender. Add a pinch of salt and pepper to your taste. Pour the egg mixture to the saucepan and gently stir. Top with grated mozzarella cheese. Bake at 350 degrees F for 5 minutes then serve and enjoy.

33. The Best French toast

Ingredients:

1 loaf of bread

4 eggs

½ cup milk

Dash of salt and pepper

½ tsp. vanilla extract

2 tbsp. olive oil

½ tsp. cinnamon

¼ cup maple syrup

How to Prepare:

Pour the olive oil on a large frying pan and place on medium heat. Whisk the eggs, milk, salt and vanilla together in a medium bowl with a flat bottom. Slice the loaf of bread into ½ inch thick slices. Dip each slice into the egg mixture on the flat bottom allowing it to rest in the mixture on both sides for 2 seconds. Then place each dipped bread slice on the large frying pan and cook until they are light brown on both sides and set aside. Serve with maple syrup or cinnamon and enjoy.

34. Cod Fish Special

Ingredients:

1 lb. of codfish filets

1 tbsp. olive oil

1 lemon, sliced

½ cup of capers

1 sliced onion

1 small can of black olives sliced

1 small tomato sliced

Flour to coat the filets

How to Prepare:

Line a large baking dish with the cod filets that have been coated with flour. Place the sliced onion, black olives, tomato slices, capers on top and around the cod filets and then drizzle everything with the olive oil.

Cover with aluminum foil and bake for 10 minutes at 350 degrees F. Remove foil and bake for another 2 minutes. Serve warm with lemon on the side.

35. Stuffed Cod

Ingredients:

6 cod filets

1 cup cooked spinach

1 cup bread crumbs seasoned

½ cup Parmesan cheese

1 egg

1 lemon, sliced

1 tbsp. olive oil

How to Prepare:

In a medium bowl, mix the cooked spinach with the seasoned bread cubes, egg, and parmesan cheese until uniform and firm texture is reached. Spoon out a tablespoon of the spinach mixture and place on the center of each fillet. Carefully wrap the filet around the mixture. Place in a large oven pan and drizzle with olive oil and hint of salt and pepper. Bake for 15 minutes at 350 degrees F. Cod should flake when touched with a fork. Serve with lemon on the side and enjoy.

36. Orange Cod

Ingredients:

4 cod filets

1 sliced blood orange

½ tsp. garlic powder

1 tbsp. olive oil

Hint of salt and pepper

1 lemon, sliced

How to Prepare:

Arrange the cod filets on an 8 x 12 baking dish. Add a hint of salt and pepper and garlic powder. Sprinkle with olive oil and bake for 8 minutes at 350 degrees F. Remove from oven and top with the slices of blood orange. Complete cooking for 2 additional minutes until cod flakes when touched with a fork. Serve with lemon on the side and enjoy.

37. Baked Cod Fish

Ingredients:

4 cod filets

1 tbsp. olive oil

1 small tomato, sliced

1 small lemon, sliced

1 tsp. chili powder

Hint of salt and Pepper

How to Prepare:

Layer filets in a baking dish and cover with slices of tomatoes, onion, and lemon.

Drizzle with olive oil and salt, pepper and chili powder. Bake uncovered for 10 minutes at 350 degrees F.

38. Tuna Melt

Ingredients

1 can of tuna, in oil

4 slices mozzarella cheese

1 sliced tomato

4 Croissants

1 tsp. olive oil

How to Prepare:

Heat the olive oil on a skillet on low heat. Slice the croissants and place the bottom slice on the pan with the tender area facing up. Spread each of the 4 croissant bottom slices on the tender side with a slice of mozzarella cheese, a slice of tomato, and tuna. Then drizzle some olive oil on top. Cover each bottom slice with the top slice of the croissant and flip holding both side of the sandwich. Cook until the cheese melts and enjoy.

39. Turkey pepperoni Egg Scramble

Ingredients:

4 eggs slightly beaten

¼ cup milk

6 slices turkey pepperoni, precooked

1 small pepper diced

1 small onion chopped into small pieces

1 tbsp. olive oil

Salt and pepper

How to Prepare:

In a small bowl, beat the eggs. Then heat the olive oil on a medium-sized frying pan at low heat. Sauté the onions, peppers, and turkey pepperoni slices until tender. Add the eggs and the milk, and mix in the pan until uniform. Cook until egg scramble is tender to your taste.

ADDITIONAL TITLES FROM THIS AUTHOR

70 Effective Meal Recipes to Prevent and Solve Being Overweight: Burn Fat Fast by Using Proper Dieting and Smart Nutrition

By

Joe Correa CSN

48 Acne Solving Meal Recipes: The Fast and Natural Path to Fixing Your Acne Problems in Less Than 10 Days!

By

Joe Correa CSN

41 Alzheimer's Preventing Meal Recipes: Reduce or Eliminate Your Alzheimer's Condition in 30 Days or Less!

By

Joe Correa CSN

70 Effective Breast Cancer Meal Recipes: Prevent and Fight Breast Cancer with Smart Nutrition and Powerful Foods

By

Joe Correa CSN

www.ingramcontent.com/pod-product-compliance
Lightning Source LLC
Chambersburg PA
CBHW052048070526
44584CB00017B/2097